MODERN RASPUTIN

MODERN RASPUTIN

POEMS BY

ROSA LYSTER

UHLANGA

2016

Modern Rasputin

© Rosa Lyster, 2016, all rights reserved

Published in Cape Town, South Africa by uHlanga in 2016

uhlangapress.co.za

Distributed outside South Africa by African Books Collective

africanbookscollective.com

ISBN: 978-0-620-73322-9

Edited by Nick Mulgrew

Cover photograph by Allan Morran

Cover lettering by Alice Edy

Proofread by Rebecca Houston and Jennifer Jacobs

The body text of this book is set in

Garamond Premier Pro, 10.5PT on 16PT

Grateful acknowledgement to the following publications
in which versions of the following poems were first published:
"IN ANSWER TO THE QUESTION...", "The Zoo in the War", and
"The first ghost is a policeman" on *The Toast*; "Don't ask me to explain how
this works" on *The Awl*; and "The Last Road Dogs" on *Aerodrome*.

ACKNOWLEDGEMENTS

One found poem in this collection comes from the "Ithaca" episode of *Ulysses* by James Joyce; another is composed from answers to first-year English exam questions on Albert Camus' *The Plague* and Zadie Smith's *On Beauty*.

The title to "IN ANSWER TO THE QUESTION: WHAT SCENES WOULD ONE LIKE TO HAVE FILMED" is taken from Vladimir Nabokov's *Strong Opinions*.

The cover photograph, of my mother (back cover) and her best friend (front cover), was taken by Allan Morran. The photograph on page 73 was taken by Jarred Figgins.

Thank you to my editor, Nick, who makes all of this very easy, and who often understands my work better than I do.

Thank you to everyone at *Prufrock*, especially Helen.

To my family and my pals: I love all of you so much it's embarrassing.

Four of the poems in here are composed of emails between me and my friends, so special thanks to Matthew, Sarah, Frith, and Rom, for being such excellent people, and for always saying such excellent things, and for letting me turn those things into poems.

Thank you to Rom, again, and Ben, for reading so many of these poems, and for being on my side.

Thank you to Jarred, the no. 1 modern Rasputin.

Thank you to Simon and Mae, who I miss too much.

Thank you to my brother, who has made me laugh for 30 years.

Thank you to Caitie, who I met on the stairs.   –R.L.

For my parents,
who show me what life is supposed to be like.

CONTENTS

Don't ask me to explain how this works

Our bathroom tap makes you electrocuted.
Don't ask me to explain how this works.

You need to wear shoes with rubber soles
to brush your teeth
or to stand bent over the sink at four a.m.
so thirsty you could bite something, or die;
or wake up the person in your bed
to say that you are thinking about tearing your face off.

    (Because what's going on here?

    This whole demented street parade,
    with the brass band composed of teenage girls
    who are not very good at the trumpet,
    and the man shooting fireworks out of his bedroom window,
    and the two of us in the middle, unable to do anything
    but walk staring straight ahead and trying not to scream.

    All that?
    I can't do it.)

Sometimes the tap will take you by surprise
and you will jerk back your head
and say fuck over and over into your bathroom door.
Other times you will think,   *well, of course*

I expected nothing less from this life than to be shocked
over and over
and to try to light a cigarette while I am already smoking one
and to try to text the person sleeping in my bed
while I am looking at their face
and say that I am thinking about moving to a mountain
with a very powerful telescope at the top
and never speaking to you again – just staring at you
through my telescope and trying to smoke
two cigarettes at once.

I once told a friend that I was incapable
of truly being hurt – like, shot with a crossbow hurt –
because I just didn't care enough. She laughed
and pulled up her sleeve to show me three evil roses –
three little scars in the bend of her elbow –
and said "I did that with a cigarette.
You just haven't met the right person yet."

When my ex-girlfriend was six
she made a list of what mattered to her most.
Here is the list:

- school
- friends
- art
- money
- fear
- food
- health

She was six and even then she knew
that fear comes before food
and that as you get older
(and walk down Kloof Street crying
and trying to smoke two cigarettes at once
and you are totally unrecognisable
to yourself, well) fear just keeps moving up the list.
And you get more and more scared and fear beats art
like paper beats rock,
and you stand over the sink at four a.m.
and your feet are bare

and here comes the shock
and your hands grip the tap
because they cannot help it
and you think, *well, of course.*

Fire-eater

Want to hear a good joke?
Want to hear everything I know about Russian prisons?
There is one called Butyrka and there are stories you wouldn't believe:
people screaming uncontrollably
and some other things that you are better off not knowing.

Want to hear about the time my brother and his friend Drew got into a fight?
This guy held a set of car keys up to my brother's neck
and a whole lot of other stuff that I cannot recall
because I only heard the story once
before I filed it away for later use.

Want to hear about some dumb shit I saw on Twitter?
Want to hear about the time someone I know shot a horse?
Just dispatched a grey horse with a gun?

Want to hear about my flight? It was packed
with people who work in advertising.

(They were all hungover and shaking.
The air in the plane smelled vaguely of chemicals.
Imagine if they had all started puking together.
Just all of them, all down on all fours in the aisle.
This did not happen but imagine it did.)

I feel like a fire-eater.
I feel like someone set a fire
and then poured it into me
and now it's there and you can see it.
Trees five metres apart burst into flame, the river begins to boil.

Want to hear about my friend Caitie's baby?
Want to hear about how Mae and I once stood
in an empty restaurant kitchen and asked
each other if we were birds?
I feel like how Bunny Wailer must feel

every minute of the day.
Just a fire-eater. Just the whole forest aflame.

Want to know how amazing I think peacocks are?
We do not deserve them,
we do not speak of them enough.
We should give them a country,
we should put them in every movie we make from now on.

I wake up and start talking immediately
because there is so much to tell you.
I have tried drinking water.

I am having a lot of baths
and going swimming in the rain.
I drank a litre of grape juice standing in my parents' kitchen.
If I open my mouth very wide,
you might hear the crackling.
Is this what fire-eaters feel like?

Is this OK?

Me and the Colonel

That week, they told us both to find a poem by a woman
and teach it to our first-year classes, mostly girls of eighteen
who still loved Harry Potter and who drew back bitten from "One Art",
because *why should it all be so negative all the time,*
and *not everything ends in disaster now does it.*

I decided on "The Colonel", just to get away from love.
(Though I thought of the man who had brought her there,
who told her with his eyes to say nothing, and she listened,
and how later they'd fucked in his jeep while those dogs barked
and barked, and how he called it making love.)

You didn't want to choose – there were no good women poets,
you said – but you supposed "The Goblin Market" would be alright
for these girls of eighteen who had crunched up next to each other
at boarding school; who mouthed along to *The Notebook* and scorched
each other's hair, and stared at each other like poets did.

We loved "The Colonel", they said, but it's not a real poem.
Where are the stanzas and where is her opened heart, her baby?
You laughed and said they hated "The Goblin Market"
like I wouldn't believe – one girl snapped her laptop shut;
said *tell me why this is better than Harry Potter.*

It made me need to smoke, and so the two of us stood
under the Arts Block ledge and argued.
You kept smiling and I kept trying to think
of the reason I was there. I was laughing, you said,
because it's true: there are no good women poets.

Deep down, you said, I knew that I don't like women poets;
I was one of those girls who other girls can't seem to like.

And deep down I knew that I was laughing because it was true.

Snow White

Two separate men have given me apples.
Sleeping with me, then giving me apples.

The first time a whole bag; the other
a single Pink Lady, which rolled around in
my bag until I ate it in an Uber
three days later as the driver told me a
joke I only realised was demeaning to
women another three days later, after
swimming lengths at the Long Street Baths.

The joke relied on the apparently widely-held belief
that women are lazy –
do people really say that?
(The world is a very strange place, and
people will say and do anything. I heard
there are men having sex with horses now.
I heard Taylor Swift doesn't have a belly button.)

I think the driver might have been a professional magician
at some point in his undoubtedly troubled life.
He just had that air about him.

(Once I saw a man with an Illuminati tattoo at Robberg,
an extremely genial Italian with the triangle and the eye
on his arm. God alone knows what sort of feverish nonsense
someone like that is dreaming up every minute of the day.
He probably has a tattoo saying
"WOMEN ARE A BURDEN ON THE STATE"
in the space where his belly button should be.)

The world is a very strange place
and probably I should not worry.
I do, though.

My worry now is that the apple thing is like the joke:
that I will only understand it later
at some unspecified point;
after swimming lengths at the Long Street Baths.
I worry that one day the apple thing will be revealed to me
in all its fulsome weirdness; that I will finally understand
its true and illuminating significance.

Apples: what do they mean.
Apples: why did those two men
look at me and think
this woman needs an apple at once.
Apples: what is this about, please.

One day I will be swimming lengths
and I will see that the apples
were their way of telling me
that I am secretly a horse,
or something to do with original sin,
or that they wanted to poison me,
à la the witch in *Snow White*.

I could also be reading into this
a little too much. Besides,
I have always loved apples:
it would be nice to think
that they could see this on my face.

The Last Road Dogs

Challenge extended:
we wonder, would you spend an afternoon
in the dark and foreign corners
of the Wikipedia category "Australian Criminals"?

It offers no surprises –
they are a loose and unhinged people after all
that has happened there:
the men, the flies, proximity to the sun.

They make up a considerable percentage
of the internationally-imprisoned.
They traffic in amphetamines on a regular basis;
in jail they write *Shantaram*.

I knew immediately
that I could spend a whole afternoon
reading the statements of the accused
to myself in an Australian accent.

> The courtroom is packed,
> the woman on the stand looks left, looks right
> at the man who will not look at her,
> and says *yes it's him*.

Yes, he is one of Melbourne's main dealers
in what the papers refer to as "party drugs".
There's a scar on his face that I gave him.
We were road dogs together, I admit it.

This is how the underworld speaks
in Australia today:
like a Charles Manson interview
I once read on a plane.

The jury reels back as one
at the road dog's admission.
The verdict is sealed – they don't care
about what happens now.

She leaves the courtroom
and he walks past her shackled in the passage,
wearing a stripy uniform and a hat with corks on,
the scar that she gave him still vivid.

She had mugged him for a joke outside a party
to show which one of them was meaner.
One minute was *I love you*,
the next dragging her keys in his face.

They brush past each other
like the corks on his hat.
He into the dark and she into the day;
he the only road dog she would ever come to love.

Another two trees

What can you draw?
I can draw a town and I can draw some people
with their faces pressed to the glass,
and their juddering worried knees
as they look out the windows of a bus.

I can't draw hair
so they are all wearing hats
and the same expression
of cautious joy,
because that's how I feel most of the time.

And because their luck has changed –
at last, they are leaving the town
for good –
they do not wave. I hate drawing hands and besides,
there is no one they care to say goodbye to.

Anyway, what else can you draw?
A river.
What kind of a river?
Just the usual river
starting at the top of the mountain.

Can you draw the mountain?
No.
You have to just imagine the sun and the wind
and how it feels to be one of two trees up there
too far apart to do anything but shout.

They try to keep up, the trees,
but the river washes their voices away
and it's awkward to wail out your feelings
at the top of your tree lungs.
It's hard. They are easily embarrassed:

they drop all their leaves at once,
which is the tree way of blushing.
They cannot stand to see each other naked like that so
mostly they are content to be quiet and pretend it's enough
that the other one is only barely out of reach.

It goes on like this for years:
they grow rings of silence around themselves,
until the bus pulls up to the mountain's foot
and the people pile out and point
to the top and adjust their hats.

They start to climb in silence
as steeply the path rises before them
and they dip their hats in the river
to stay cool – I saw this in a movie once –
while they stare at each other's bald heads and smile

cautiously, joyfully, and with apprehension.
They cannot believe they have made it out here
and that they are allowed to rest their backs
against one of the two trees and shake
their heads against the rush of the river.

Both trees bow their heads at the same time
and say could you just give this
to that tree over there. It's only a letter.
It's been a long time since
we've had company up here.

All towns have buses
with people on the road to somewhere else.
All rivers drown out voices.
All mountains have two trees at the top
trying to make themselves heard.

All letters say the same thing,
which is that I miss you and I hope
that you are fine where you are
and that if I could grow myself to touch you
then that's what I would do.

Found poem for Sarah

Someone once said that I had a lot of charm, but by then I had already left the party.
Of course, the point of a party is to make ten men fall in love with you (at least),
but we are tired and allergic and we worry about small, small things, so
I just made an error of judgement. Please forgive me. I should have stayed.
We would have held hands all the way home, going for walks and doing outings and

deciding that it is not necessary to be a grumpy, flaky bat. I feel quite blue about it.
I don't even know why, but I do. He would be a man who would open his mouth
real wide even if there is not much on his fork. (Don't tell anyone who might tell him.)
I would have to get a job in a gallery to please him, and drink wine fast, tilt my head back a lot.
It would have to be like a thing in a film with a Victorian gentleman who likes "mischief":

I would have to send texts about tunnels and sexy teeth and kissing without pause for two hours.

We would buy feathers in the morning, so thin and covered in bruises and ready for anything;

we would wear small dresses and pretend that there is a zoo to visit in this country

where there is a huge, huge fox clicking around on its toenails and trying to make friends.

We could arrive late to a silly party dressed like someone weird's idea of a bird.

Some marriages have been built on less.

First-years

During a phone call to the house of his enemy,
he speaks to the son of his enemy,
even though he is fully conscious of its futility.
He is a 57-year-old white American.
He is a fanatic poetry lover.
He is a school dropout who actively thinks he is a gangster.
He is aware of the tensions that arise when certain things are intermingled.
He is love with a girl called Victoria.
His name is Jeremy.

During a phone call to the house of his enemy,
he speaks to the son of his enemy,
about the rates, the plague, and the telegrams;
about the eleven official languages decorating the South African flag;
about the metaphysical problem that is life;
about the Nazis invading France
(although this is not as bad as it was years ago, it still happens);
about the Robin Hood-like Haitian fugitives;
and the difficulties of entrapment, death, and so forth.

If we analyse the text with a microscope,
we will see that during the phone call to the house of his enemy,
Jeremy realises he has made a terrible mistake.
If we analyse the text with a macroscope,
we will see that during the phone call to the house of his enemy,
he realises that the sequence of life is meaningless and that

the only choice is death or death.

(This needn't be a problem.)

During a phone call to the house of his enemy,

he has a falling out with Mike, Victoria's sister,

about a group of suburban children at the record store,

and other Negro-related aspects of the text.

It seems that something has been lost in translation,

but I can confidently assert that

the rats indicate Algerians during the occupation of France;

the rats represent the Jews;

the rats cannot communicate with humans and therefore

the rats represent the Nazi occupation of French Algeria.

Everything ends where it began, and vice versa.

All children can be symbolic of all children,

and they know that to define something is to do the opposite of what is meant.

There is a fancy French term for this effect – it escapes me now,

but perhaps in France formality of speech is not an issue.

Careful analysis is the only antidote to this confusion.

Let us begin.

IN ANSWER TO THE QUESTION: WHAT SCENES
WOULD ONE LIKE TO HAVE FILMED

I   Dickie Greenleaf and Tom sit for hours at the bar –
it's the one that I think is in Naples.
Tom says he is sorry for the scene on the boat;
Dickie laughs and says, please, these things happen.

II   A hand peels out from the crack in the rocks.
Miranda returns thin, but happy.
Her hair is a mess, she is tanned and she shines.
The school stands around her, all clapping.

III   Sebastian Flyte on a boat in the sun.
He sings to the man on the jetty,
"You are my rich and kind boyfriend now.
I love you and we should get married."

IV   Leonard Bast jerks up straight in the chair where he sleeps.
He shakes his head twice, he shivers:
it's clear to him now – that family's the *worst*.
He cannot see what he was thinking.

v   At the start of all drug films to ever exist,
     where they're all on the beach and they're golden –
     the whole thing is like this, just for hours and hours.
     Overdoses aren't real. No one dies or gets older.

vi   Frank O'Hara's awake in the hospital,
     his room full of beeps and white flowers.
     A nurse comes in – her vibrations are bad.
     She hates gays and fun, and his visitors.

     She says, "That's what happens when you're at Fire Island.
     You almost get killed by a *buggy*.
     Imagine how awful, imagine the shame.
     I don't like you, but get real – you are forty."

     The nurse will be taught a hard lesson, of course.
     She will learn what it means to be kind.
     They fight, her and Frank, but there's something he likes,
     and when he gets home he will call her.

     She will come to New York on a visit, and stay.
     She'll discover her cool in a crisis.
     She'll move in with this guy who laughs all the time,
     who'll turn out to be a famous sound artist.

Frank dies an old man in the house that he built.
The nurse sings a song at his wake.
Her voice is so pure – no one knew before this –
and the sound artist is pleased with his choice.

Famous children

Maybe I need to stop feeling like I am either dead or too alive,
talking so much and telling my worst story,
which is something that happened and which isn't really very funny at all,
but which I now tell to tables full of people on cocaine,
and which they will not remember the next day.
Cocaine is like that –

I'll remember it, though,
because I'm like that.

When I was little I thought Leonard Cohen was my friend,
and that *Graceland* was about my mother's first marriage,
and that I was the kid in the poster for *The Kid*.
I thought I was famous and everyone knew
I was the most important child to ever be born.
I was like that.

My best friend once tried to explain fame
to her children – they are three and five.
(To me they are famous
but never mind that.)
She told them it meant that everyone knew your name,
which is fine as explanations go.

But when they are older and they have seen people on cocaine
behaving as if they are the middle of the world,
and as if there is no picture which would not be improved
with a head-and-shoulders shot of themselves,
and as if Leonard Cohen is their best friend
and *Graceland* is about their mother;

when her children are sitting in a bar with a rock in their chest
telling a terrible story about something that happened
and which should not be used as conversational ammunition –
especially not to a table full
of people on cocaine
who will not remember any of it the next day;

when they have done all that,
I'll ask them if they remember being told about fame
for the first time.
We'll agree that it must be like being permanently on cocaine
feeling as if you are the middle of the world.
The most important child to ever be born.

We'll agree that the thing to do
is to stand up and take home the rock in your chest;
take home the terrible story about something that happened
and which really isn't very funny at all
and remember that other people are on cocaine.
Other people are famously important children.

And they will not remember any of this the next day.
(Although we will,
because we are like that.)

Found poem for Frith

1   Sometimes I am in a boat and I stretch my hands up into the trees,
and the trees are full of spiders passed out with cocaine headaches.

She was in a field and a steam train made of leaves and branches went past her.
She was in the bath at her first husband's house in a bombed European city.

She is a perfect angel. He said, "Just get pregnant."
He said, "Smoking is a privilege, and not a right."

He flung his stupid arm across her and said, "Move back."
He just kept saying, "I'm listening,"

She hears cows walking down a cobbled street,
Lindsay Lohan crying behind a door.

The clear sound of water dripping in a cave.
Lonely old men crying on the massage table.

Factories producing too many left shoes and not enough right.

II It's too funny not to tell. I bailed on Studio 54,
met Basquiat in the street. He invited me home to take drugs
but I said No Thank You, it gives me a dying sensation.
I do not need to be liberated by the desert.

I came back from Woodstock like, "That was boring."
I went home and stared at myself in the mirror for twenty minutes,
feeling everything that other people feel,
just being a person the way a leopard is a leopard.

III   From very small she expected the world
to be weird and terrible and look:

she was right, she has a limp.

IV   He is not a smart man but a terrible old HUSK and he wants her to
come home and have his beautiful children.

There are some people that you are always going to drink a lot of drinks with,
like some people were Doors fans before they ever heard the Doors.

In their mind they can see spaceships and gods and a real-life Anubis.
She thought her life would be perfect if he just bucked up

and effed her on the filing cabinet but they are married to their work,
and he has a bad car manner.

v   You spend many hours worrying that you are a sociopath or the symbol of a compassionate state or an epic miracle and I suppose that is pretty much the story.

The Queen's Hotel in summer

Dinner gong.
A glass summerhouse with tropical palms.
Young woman enters (evening dress):
a pleasant surprise at relaxed walking pace.

Stephen Dedalus, professor and author
and eccentric public laughing stock,
rests in a stuffed easychair with stout arms extended.
He sits. He is abandoned.

A young woman enters radiant.
With her is the infirm dog Athos.
Stephen Dedalus, the professor and author,
looks on them both with satisfaction.

Outside, the heaventree of stars and the humid nightblue fruit
and here is the dog (infirm) and
the young woman (sitting).
She is weary. She has travelled.

Dinner gong.
Stephen Dedalus, alone and with unmixed feeling,
comes from his dark corner and stands
beside the young woman and the dog infirm.

What did they do?
Nothing. No sound but the peal of the hour of the night
by the chime of the bells in the church in the square.
The young woman (still sitting) thinks, writes on hotel paper.

She stands. She goes to the window and
there are the stars and the fruit (nightblue).
Now, wheels and hoofs – she hurries out,
and Athos and Stephen are left behind.

The eccentric public laughing stock seizes
the solitary paper. Did he show it to Athos?
Yes. What did Athos comprehend?
Everything and everything: nothing or less.

The King and the woman who is not the Queen

Could I interest you in the existence
of the phrase "acknowledged bastard"?
An acknowledged bastard is when a king has a baby
with a woman who is not the queen.

Maybe they are in love or maybe it is something
worse than being in love –
although I am at a loss to describe
what that something might be.

There is nothing worse than being in love.
It's Anton Chigurh standing there with that cow-stunning machine,
saying, *Could you just look here for a minute, please.*

Could I interest you in the fact
that the cows don't die straight away?
They are merely knocked out in order to facilitate
easier passage to the conveyor belt.
That's what being in love is.

The king knows this but
what do you want him to do about it?
He is in love and she is in love and they are both
standing there with the bolt at their foreheads
and getting ready to travel up that conveyor belt
and through the door.

No one talks about what goes on behind there,
but everyone knows.

The king and the woman who is not the queen,

she also knows.

But they are doubled over with laughter

in the supermarket

and they are agreeing with everything the other one says

even before they say it.

And they are pushing back the hair out of one another's eyes

and she is hoping he won't mind if she just bites his shoulder

and breaks the skin.

And he hopes she won't care when he wakes her up in the middle of the night

because he misses her in his dreams.

I can't believe I met you.

You got born and then I met you,

and what are the chances of that?

So they are going to have a baby,

and that's what an acknowledged bastard is.

You can call it a "royal" bastard if you need,
but I like "acknowledged" better
because it highlights the important thing:
that everyone knows.

The king and the woman who is not the queen
would like to get married,
but everyone knows it doesn't work like that.
Soon they will have a fight.
She will look at him with pure stunning contempt –
a bolt of contempt –
and the king will remember that he had forgotten
that there is nothing worse than being in love.

(The acknowledged bastard will grow up
in a house with a garden and a horse
who sometimes sticks its head through the kitchen window.
    And that's nice.

His father will put him in charge of the post offices

and of maps

and will allow him to create three laws –

whatever he likes.

These are the perks of being a bastard.

He decides to make it a crime

to be in love with someone

and to say the words

I can't believe I met you

You got born and then I met you,

and what are the chances of that?

The punishment is you get shot out of a cannon.

He takes the law to his father the king,

and the king tells him that he is not, of course,

the first person to have tried this.

Everyone knows that there is nothing worse than being in love but the legislation will never be pushed through the courts.

And anyway, the punishment is built-in:

you get shot out of a cannon regardless;

you get Anton Chigurh coming right up and saying,

Could you just look here for a minute, please.

And you know what is coming

behind that door,

but you stand there regardless and take it.

Soon

a princess will fall in love with someone

who she knows to be a bastard – it's acknowledged.

But what do you want her to do about it?

Despite its being a crime he will fall in love with her back,

and everyone knows exactly where this is headed.

But we all just stand there and take it.)

Found poem for Romney

He was wearing this kind of a suit,
which buttons up to the neck and goes down to the floor.
It is, I suppose, a kind of a dress for a man,
like what Sun Ra would wear when he was asleep.

He'd spent the whole night talking to a really great prostitute,
who was bathed in that golden light we've all heard
so much about. He said to her, "You are a gift,
and if you went to war I would follow you."

It's just a true fact that her last name is Snowball.
He knows. A thing he does not know is that sometimes
she likes to go out and dance her little socks off,
guns blazing, deceptively tall (maybe a giant).

She views him with a distant benevolence.
A patrician. It's true that her work is meaningless.
She offers him a lobster and taps on the tank
to ask those guys whether they are OK in there.

She has a blog with a tab for "Confessions".
The first confession is how to dig a hole –
is this not an admission of something?
The lobsters try without success to remember.

They are all of them bathed in that golden light
we've heard so much about – her, him, and the lobsters.
He undoes a button of the Sun Ra night suit.
The lobsters have seen this movie before.

Found poem for Matthew

I'm sorry I got you involved in a conversation that showed
no clear sign of ever ending ever,
about Honey People and the science-fiction post-cyberpunk novel,
about being in a water taxi with Margaret Atwood.
Maybe I hate all artists now and that's it forever.

His voice is this raspy, thin little whisper and he also does calligraphy.
He decided to stand on a chair to better conduct himself.
I saw that young ballroom dancer sashay up to him and say
that the only way to come into Venice is via the sea.
The chair broke underneath him and he dropped like a stone.

His voice and his body are these two entirely distinct entities,
and possibly when he stood back up he said sorry.
I saw that young ballroom dancer sashay up to him and say
that calling someone a naai is the funniest thing to ever exist;
a person saying that, and believing it in their hearts to be true.

I'm sorry I got you involved in a conversation about the Freemasons,
and unthinkable wealth, and one of my best poets,
and some photographs of them in the house of Homi Bhabha.
You are completely right. It's pretty real. I'm sorry, so
tell me everything you learned and everything you found out, please.

You give me one good reason why I cannot stand outside the UCT club
and mug someone. This must have already happened.
It would be like finding two hundred rand in a pocket or something.
I would take that key for his new Mustang and stick it into his arm
like a needle and everyone would fear me for being so Tough.

I was up too late reading his diary – I think he has a lot of Pain.
The last line! He said that he saw that young ballroom dancer
sashay up and tell him not to stand on any chairs, I guess.
He definitely stares out of a hotel window in the early hours of dawn.
Maybe I hate all artists now and that's it forever.

Your mother and I
for Goldie

I hope you sleep like you are in a competition.
I hope you beat all the other babies
at being asleep.

You get hoisted up onto the podium at the end –
FIRST PLACE FOR SLEEPING –
and you don't know really what's happening,

but it just feels right.

You wave.
You ruffle the pages of a magazine.
(All babies like to do this.)

You point fixedly at something not very interesting,
something like a handbag.
You say your first word:

it's "bird."

I hope one day
you look at your parents and say that you need to learn
an instrument that will embarrass your mother.

Something like the trumpet.

I hope you play it every morning
and that you march up and down the passage
with your chin held high and with wild exhilaration.

Here you are, nerd, walking up the stairs
after your first trumpet recital.
I hope you have a very heavy tread.

I hope your socks are falling down,
and your hair is escaping the clutches of the plait
your mother taught herself to give you.

She's in the car, your mum. Maybe
she is smoking a guilty cigarette or maybe
texting me to say *I can't believe I have a child who plays the trumpet.*

I can't believe I get to be her mum.

You are nearly at the top of the stairs
when you see a kid whose hair is also
on the move, and whose socks are falling down.

She has to lean right back
to look you in the eye.
You both stand there and she says hi.

Then you say something to make her laugh
and she says something to make you look around
and think *I can't believe there are two of us.*

You look around and think *well, that was easy.*

I hope you are little when it happens.
Your mother and I were big – we were nineteen
and twenty when we met at the top of the stairs.

By the time we hit the bottom we belonged to each other.
It really was that easy,
like almost nothing else is.

I'm sorry about the world, baby.

I'm sorry we have not yet figured out how to legislate
against anyone being sad, or hungry, or scared.
I'm sorry we have not managed to make it illegal

for us to hurt each other.

Try not to think about it too much.
Try to play your trumpet
in a way that makes your mother scream with delight.

You're lucky, baby, I can feel it.
You meet your best friend at the top of the stairs one day
and by the time you hit the bottom

you belong to each other.

Parent material

I fetch Grace every day from school.
She knows everything.
She wears a cap and she is eight and the other day
I watched her stick her hands into a letter-box –
both hands – and I told her it was illegal
to steal someone's post. She said, "I'm a tiny criminal.
People think I'm a kid because I don't pay taxes."
Grace knows about taxes and she knows
what kind of bird she is (a flamingo),
and how to draw a picture of me and her
sitting on our respective elephants
underneath a rainbow.

You feel that a limit has been reached.
A wall has been breached or taken apart,
brick by brick.
You feel like an instrument
unscrewed into its component parts
left rattling round the bottom of a suitcase.
A shitty instrument, like a recorder,
never to be put back together.
You feel final and you feel absolutely
that no good can come from what is afoot here.
What idiot, what incompetent
left you in charge of your life?

But then you sail down Geneva Drive,
and there is the sea,
and here are the daisies outside the school gate
and two little girls pushing back their fringes –
"This is my sister and I am my sister's sister" –
and boys smacking each other full in the face with their schoolbags,
and there is Grace in her cap and her ponytail,
and she tells you about crystals and she listens
when you tell her to put on her seatbelt or to hold your hand
as you cross the road together, and
what idiot, what incompetent,
would not pull herself together?

You bump into people when they are not expecting it
and you walk away worried that you have left
a permanent and unsettling impression.
You are heading for some kind of limit, or another.
You are repeatedly crashing through
walls meant to stand forever.
You are a recorder rattling around
in the bottom of a suitcase,
dismantled and likely to stay that way.
You talk too much about stuff that can not matter, and
what idiot, what incompetent
would not say that you need to take it easy?

But then here comes Grace
and she wants to be a geologist.
She knows about parent material
and consolidated rock and soil horizons.
She knows everything and she listens
when you tell her to hold your hand or that it is a crime
to stick your hands into a letter-box and steal someone's post.
She knows everything but she is small and you are big, and

what idiot, what incompetent,
would not pull herself together?

The first ghost is a policeman

She is
downcast, she is far down at heart.
And she has this new young crowd of ghosts,
just standing around her and tapping the walls,
swinging the cupboards wide open at night,
full of epic lust and jabbering with anxiety.

One ghost
is the acknowledged bastard of Henry VIII.
He plays the recorder under her floorboards,
and makes the sound of a sleeping bag unzipping.
He has sworn to accompany her
all of the minutes there are.

There is
no point in having a forest
if you are too scared to go in it.
So she takes the ghosts with her,
like she has a choice.

One ghost
was a goddess – the loveliest thing.
The fish when they saw her forgot about swimming,
the giraffes bent their necks to the ground.
The trees dropped their fruit and the birds cried hot tears.
Her name when she had one was Iris.

One ghost
wishes she could live without girls
for a little while and just be happy,
alone in her part of the house,
like that is possible.

There is
a ghost that is only a smell
of gin and cocaine and the blooming tobacco flowers
that she assumes the ghosts like to look at.
A breeze down the back of her jacket;
a cold little hand's swipe at her neck.

One is
the lord of a warring state.
But no ghost around here will fight him.
He runs his sword against the railings instead,
waves it above his ghostly head and hopes
that it will provoke a challenge. But
the ghosts round here are bored of dying.

Only one
she knows is bad for sure.
He will tear them both to
pieces completely if she would just let him.
He says she will wait 'til she cries herself blind,
'til she cries her eyes right out of her head.
And then he will sit on the end of her bed,
and talk to her quietly about her mistakes.

She stands
on the bank,
and watches the ghosts all in a line,
getting their ghost knees wet as they cross the river.
The trees of the forest are all dark behind her.
The water is hissing like snakes.

Modern Rasputin

for JF

If you were in any doubt
as to whether the two of us
gave each other matching tattoos last night,
let me put your mind at rest:
yes.

The world is divided between people
who think this is fun
and people who think that this is a situation
requiring the intervention
of a professional.

The world is divided between people
who don't wake up and think about Rasputin
on an almost daily basis
and those of us who do.
RASPUTIN.

The world is divided between people
who get a real fucking kick out of just staring at his name
and people who wouldn't even look at a picture of him
given the opportunity.
RASPUTEY.

The tattoos were easy:
you just lie there and you let someone
stick a needle into you over and over.
It hurts but what doesn't?
It hurts but what would Rasputin do?

He would tell you that this world is a genuinely nightmarish place.
There is Isis now and in Beirut I heard
that the refugees have a curfew
so that the tourists don't have to look at them for too long.
Everything hurts and is getting worse all the time.

And so if someone appears bearing the possibility of fun
waving fun above their head like the flag of a country
where everyone goes to sleep laughing
about what a good time they are having,
then you must recognise the opportunity you are being given.

And you must take it.

I feel like I am violating the terms of the Geneva Convention.
I feel like someone is going to call the police, at least.
I feel like the world is divided between people
who will never speak to me again
and those who will phone me in the middle of the night

to talk about Rasputin, just about what kind of a guy he was,
and how he was certainly having sex with every last one
of those Romanovs, even the ever-contrary Olga,
the one who couldn't be a nurse because
she kept falling in love with the soldiers.

Even her and Rasputin got it on
in a major and frankly disturbing way,
the two of them lying in the back of a sleigh
under a bear fur coat, Rasputin pouring the
most messed-up sexy stuff into her aristocratic ear.

She is having so much fun,
she feels like someone is going to call the police,
or at least round up her entire family and execute them.
She knows and Rasputin knows
that none of this should be allowed.

But when someone appears waving the possibility of fun
above their head like the flag of a country
where everyone is smiling until their ears hurt
then you must take the opportunity you are being given
and tear into it.

(The tattoo says "fun", by the way.
Just little,
just at the top of my ribs;
just the very essence of what it is
to be a modern Rasputin.

The world is divided between people who think this is a good story
and people who stopped reading a long time ago.)

And somewhere in a Russian field,
Olga and Rasputin are fucking like they are being paid to do it.
And screaming with laughter.
And it will hurt but what won't?
The only thing to do, then,

is see how long they can get away with it.

The Zoo in the War

Out of all of the animals
that are left in the zoo
only the dull ones remain.

Who knows how they got in a zoo
in the first place? Dirty old bunnies
and deers with long teeth and short tempers.

Not the animals you'd pay to see.
A cane rat with fur hard like scales
all slippery and waiting to climb your arm;

mid-sized birds with no girlfriends
and no one to show off to;
some hens, a mouse, two bees.

And now here they all are:
no keepers, no food, no chance
they will figure this out on their own.

The beautiful ones were stolen
on day one, bundled into baskets
and put on the train to Paris.

They're the toast of the city. They'll be a book
that tells us how to feel about the war.
(We don't know whose side they're on, but no matter.)

The beautiful ones will not reveal
how many got left behind.
The social lions won't say, but they know.

The smart and the dumb and the nutters,
all watched as the lovelies were carried away.
And some of them saw what to do.

The smart ones pulled out their manuals
on how to escape.
Step one said: dig a hole – you're in trouble.

Step two: you don't have a choice here at all.
Step three: we are all on your side.
Step four: how are you coming along with that hole?

The thick ones are not so quick
to say that the hour has come to leave.
They will wait and see if their breakfast comes back.

Moth-eaten, they will defy you
to ask what business they have here.
A zoo is no place for a hen, two bees.

The smart ones are out.
The hole has been dug. It was easy.
(Step five just says: I told you so.)

To tell you the plight of the crazies is simple.
Mostly: tangled in the wire.
Sometimes: hit by a truck.

The dumb ones were not sorry to see them go.
No more flicking of tails like whips and
whispering that this is the end.

They know that help is coming and breakfast
will soon be upon them.
The slow ones know that panic is the enemy –

so stay calm, breathe low, and be ready to wait.

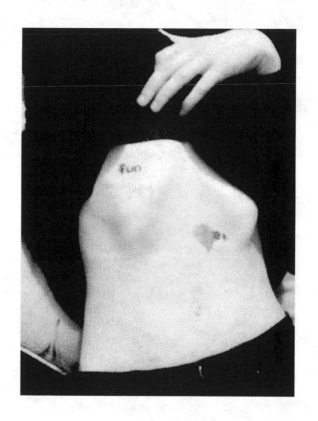

POETRY FOR THE PEOPLE

ALSO AVAILABLE:

Imbewu Yesini by The CYPHER

Prunings by Helen Moffett

Questions for the Sea by Stephen Symons

Failing Maths and My Other Crimes by Thabo Jijana
WINNER OF THE 2016 INGRID JONKER PRIZE FOR POETRY

Matric Rage by Genna Gardini
COMMENDED FOR THE 2016 INGRID JONKER PRIZE FOR POETRY

the myth of this is that we're all in this together by Nick Mulgrew

COMING IN 2017: COLLECTIONS FROM
KOLEKA PUTUMA & FRANCINE SIMON

AVAILABLE FROM GOOD BOOKSTORES IN SOUTH AFRICA
& ELSEWHERE FROM THE AFRICAN BOOKS COLLECTIVE,
IN PRINT AND DIGITAL

UHLANGAPRESS.CO.ZA

Printed in the United States
By Bookmasters